SESSIONS OF A SANDSTORM

A self-therapy.

SESSIONS OF A SANDSTORM
A SELF-THERAPY.

Isaac Miebi Mendez

QUERENCIA

Querencia Press
Chicago, Illinois

QUERENCIA PRESS

ISBN 978 1 959118 65 7

www.querenciapress.com

First Published in 2023

Querencia Press
Chicago IL

Printed & Bound in the United States of America

FOREWORD

As I delve into SESSIONS OF A SANDSTORM by Isaac Miebi Mendez, I am reminded of the words of one of Africa's most celebrated poets, Wole Soyinka, who once said, "The greatest threat to freedom is the absence of criticism." In this chapbook, Isaac Mendez offers a poignant critique of the generational curses that plague our society, stripping individuals of their identities, their heritage, and their humanity. Mendez draws from his personal experiences to paint vivid images of the pain and the turmoil that often accompany the weight of one's family legacy.

Through the collection's poems, Mendez navigates the complexities of father-son relationships, the impact of religious beliefs on family dynamics, and the struggle to find one's voice amidst the chaos. His words are raw, unfiltered, and at times, uncomfortable, as he challenges us to confront the uncomfortable truths that we would rather sweep under the rug. He exposes the wounds that have festered for far too long, reminding us that the only way to heal is to confront the past head-on.

SESSIONS OF A SANDSTORM is a brave and unapologetic exploration of the intersection between personal trauma and societal norms, especially when the vulnerability of an African man is held to the lights. It is a testament to the resilience of the human spirit and a call to action for all those who have been silenced by their circumstances. It is a reminder that the most powerful tool we have is our voice and that we must use it to break the cycle of generational curses.

Isaac Mendez is a poet whose words will linger long after the last page is turned. His chapbook is a must-read for anyone who seeks to understand the complexities of the human experience and the transformative power of words.

—GRACIANO ENWEREM (Sir Grrraciano), Multiple Award-winning Poet, Serial Author, & Teacher

To my father, you who taught me that I am not your legacy.

To personal tutor Sarah Maclannen, the one who believed & guided me.

To my one time love, Enya. you who declared therapy.

Finally, to those who wander, you are the core of a refined diamond. Stay strong as I did.

CONTENTS

PREFACE

—*Isn't life a bouquet dipped in blood?*

For those who will somehow stumble on this book, brace yourself. I think that masculine mental health discussed in poetry is rare. In fact, talking about a man's mental health and his home truths has never been easy, especially when it is done through a mirror. At some point, it felt like this book had to exist for life to go on, and because I went on, I hope that somebody out there can see reasons to go on as well.

There are times I found myself on my knees, head down, and thinking of how to find someone who I could just talk to so I didn't implode. It had to be someone who could share my skin and see through my eyes because that was the only way I truly would feel understood. Unfortunately, that never happened, but fortunately, poetry happened, and as a consequence, each poem took form. Some of the poems were incredibly hard to write, however after a while it got easier and I felt better. See? Poetry does help.

Sessions of a Sandstorm is for those struggling with a unique experience, generational trauma, patriotic shackles dragging you into an endless hole, and the inexplicable feeling that you have to find something significantly greater than the average to keep you alive in this chaotic world.

I found therapy in this chapbook. One of my hopes is for you too, who sits on the edge like I once did, to find refuge and comfort in my shared experiences.

This book explores intricately the dynamics of domestic relationships, their violence, and their sense of duty. It expands into a shared outlook of tribal challenges, and stereotypes, and finally settles in its examinations of nationalism and implications of migration.

These are home truths that I personally feel are unavoidable in day-to-day living.

—Isaac Miebi Mendez

I am not my father's son…

Natural hairs only relax when hit by the heat.
I conditioned my twisted brain to turn pain into daisies
the day a newsletter photographed my father
soaked in goat's blood with hands stretched out,
reaching for velvet skies.

I've wished I could abandon my body like a lychee
in its fruity sojourn or become the remnant of a broken spirit,
searching for ways to exhaust my bloodline,
replace my bones with clay, and dry away.
I've been a sponge purging itself of impurities
while asking myself if I am strong enough
to take on his baton and run this race.

Why do we realise our breaking point,
when the weight of our name breaks our backs?

My father has been diligently obeying the law
of cumulative returns for small defeats.
He's like a child who keeps falling
upon learning his first steps.
This time, he is staying down.
My father has lost his mind, too broke to afford
the conscience of his lost years.

This morning, under the New Year's harmattan's blue,
he wafts out to his father's grave on ten toes, chanting in *Ijaw;*
He wants to bottle his father's ghost!
Half-naked and surrounded by neighbourhood eyes,
his skinny legs still confidently march on to madness.

> *"My spirit wife is guarding four bags of cowries.*
> *My son, don't worry."*

Isn't life a bouquet dipped in blood?
Its bittersweetness has become sour this time
because my father will never be employed again.

& I know that madmen have no shame,
so I have to carry it for him.
Because I know that generational curses can't be broken

by old charms, half-baked prayers, or half-baked poems,
& I need conviction to finish this one.
I'm tired of carrying this guilt
like the invisible cloak blinding him.

How long shall sour grapes swallowed by old mouths torture milk teeth?
How long will children pay for the sins of their fathers?

#2

We see eye to eye
when he drops me off at school,
but then he tells me:
"*Your mother is a witch.*
You are not allowed to see her ever again."
Men of God could never be wrong...

Here I am, ensconced away from harsh stars,
desperately trying not to lose count
of how many times I have tried not to lose *my* mind.
Nightmares wake me up to his face at 2 am,
wishing there were a corner in this house to hide
my body in the same way that my father hides his love.

I find shelter in my mother's voice,
begging me that I have to forgive this poem.
Shivers will last until my father's fists
land on my face and his feet trek on my spine.
I have to understand that he has spent
a lifetime fighting his demons,
and I am the last man
standing.

***

I number the days when
I lay bare and exposed in the living room,
thinking of reasons to keep living
while scraping out layers, picking out scars,
and laying them by each door.
That way, I don't have to lie to my teachers
when they question my fractured skin.
There are pieces left behind that will leave a stench,
yet my father could not smell his own and yell

blood. At the house, I am banging my head on the wall,
in the same way, he does to me while telling myself:
"*It's a lie. Am I not my father's son?*"
When a war starts, nobody tells a madman...

In the aftermath of chaos, I will imagine
the lonely road of being brave.
Maybe then I can stop pressing my ears
and stop screaming in the shower,
while I wait for the water to wash his voice
down the drain.

Maybe when I sit outside,
the neighbours will take off
their pity masks as they stare.
Perhaps I could learn the looseness
of deep breaths
and not be so fucking angry anymore.
If I leave and join my mother's coven,
it could mean that I don't have to be a sandstorm
of a boy anymore...

There is no evil forest to throw away your child.

—To whom the gods want to destroy, they first make mad.

Every day I watch my father dance, showcasing
his new steps. Only he hears the hypnotic drums
and I am left with his footprints leading us
straight to his open grave.

He is a puppet strung along to his master's
tongue. Tongue-tied to their thread, it goes 'round,
& around my father's neck, choking out all his
common sense.

They say that there is no evil forest to throw
away your child. Yet, my father drags
his firstborn son through every bush,
in an attempt to banish demons fighting against him.

Tearing up my brother's bare back to give way
for deliverance. Because his cane is blessed
for purification. & my brother's clothes
were the only ones holding

the weight of his tears.
That night, I believe that the gods shut their eyes.
There were no stars to take away the darkness,
so my father could not see the truth.

Your mother sent you! Confess.
Confess…

Whipping away to a new beat.

MIGRANT

SHRINK

This moment of sifting
thoughts like saltwater
in a
            shattered glass.
I am slinking into cuts,
            dripping
blood
      on
            my knee, my wrist.

                        *

In a summer pool,
the kids play outside
only when the sun comes out
to darken their skin.
Seconds after my feet touch
the tiles, they remove themselves
from the pool.
            They shifted the smile on my face,
looked
            at me, the way children don't look
at cake or ice cream. Whispers
ripple
            from ear to ear:
                        taste of chlorine.

                        *

Santa Cruz, Manila.
            A lanky blonde
man shadowed me, watching me with dubious eyes—
as if I had reddish mud smeared on my face
and wore tattered clothes.
He leaned over the cheese shelf, murmuring

'Don't do it mate, don't do it...'
surprised by my peso on the counter.

                    *

In the eyes of my mirror,
I am too big for this small room.
Boxed
                in.
To those kids, I am not
as sweet as vanilla. To the man, I am
weird.   Gap in my front tooth,
a tiny piece of
                grit
somehow mixed up
in his plate of cooked
white beans.

Foolish Honour

In a nightclub, I maintained my aloofness under
golden flecks of light that glistened in my whisky.
Suddenly, a brunette woman approached, gate-crashing
my peace.

"Where are you from?"

"I am Nigerian."

"Wow," she responded, her eyes travelling around my face.

"I am from Watford. Sadly, not as exotic as you..."

I was the bittersweet tang that slapped
her taste buds, signalling her fuzzy brain
to prolong an uncommon thrill
only I could provide.

A possibility of being discardable.

Like sour milk spat out. It disrupted

an orthodox flavour that already

existed in her mouth.

She had branded me: OUTSIDER,
removing me from the crowd of tippling
bodies that blended my disguise.
With her tongue, she proclaimed her power.

I was not authentic enough to imitate

the tactile feel of glass clutched

to her fingers. Tap,

tap,

tap. Her finger flitted

about to pluck

an exotic fruit.

I had embodied the vodka itself,

allowing her to decide whether she wanted

to see   through

swallow

acknowledge the fact that:

all the while, this liquid was *here.*

(*Image of African slaves in 1518, being transported to the Caribbean. From the Hulton Archive*)

The Texture of Silence

Sometimes, we discuss the taste
of the night in our mouths.
In this open house given to us,
light never crawls in.

A crippling shiver has seized
our knees.
So, we stay put, joined together
like knitted sardines.

We have forgotten our eyes
and pretend to clap at mosquitoes,
so we know who comes through
the cryptic door.

When our hands don't meet,
we join palms and pray that our ears
catch the last crying echo of
the voice we cannot remember.

HUMAN TOUCH
(TRIBE)

ROOTS

Edisemi, you sat in the womb
of a black woman. Laughed at the harshness
of the sun, ordained your limbs with mud
from the waterside.
It does not matter how far you run,
the weaves you buy to bless your skull,
the time you take to roll your tongue,

You are as black as they come.

My mother always said,
no matter how light-skinned you get,
you can never be white.
Kekefiyai and *Polofiyai* might trick
the tongue, but in the end, truth prevails.

If a native girl tugs away from her waist beads,
the toughness of her 'FRO' will give her away.
The length of her attachments that straighten
her hair, pull her feet to the borders of the
west,
will not provide her crown with a different
shape.

You are as black as they come.

My people say:
No matter where a lady goes,
how she moves and dances with snow,
her taste buds and calabash might be lost,
but her bones belong to her roots.

*Kekefiyai (plantain porridge) Polofiyai (Yam porridge)

32

The men that keep their legs halfway beneath the sea

We are the creek,
sweet blemishless waters
that imitates the taste
of salty tears fetched
from river Niger herself.

Baptised on her waves
by preachers whose tongues
spit a song of glory

for soldiers that dance under
sunlight, because they conquered
the seas for their clan in daylight.

Shielded our shores on ten-toes
with spears swimming through
shadows.

The wind
whispers rumours that call our god
Indi

Indeed, the water spirits have kissed
our keel. Now, we hold our borders
like fish to water.

THE LIFE NO BALANCE

Yesterday we sent letters
to a friend. It can only greet him
when he is six feet deep, and
reads: *R.I.P. family & friends.*

Another letter listing burial
expenses in the name of last
respect. An attempt to make up
for all his lost sunsets.

A casket of ten thousand pounds
for the cold nights that witnessed
his leaking roof drool, raining down
his bedspreads—wet moon shelter.

A list of all sorts of food tattooed
on the menu, for all the times
he never was invited to our table.
He never knew the price of salt.

A park for our foreign cars that travelled
a hundred miles to witness his passing.
Even though our windows were tinted
When he tried to cross the street.

One million eyes and two hundred likes
on his picture, from hands that never
knew the weight of his tears, or patted
the skin on his bare back.

He never knew the smell of roses
or daisies, but we brought a bouquet
to his grave. Perhaps we forget,

the dead don't smell flowers...

Jailers

—The forest was shrinking, but the trees kept on voting for the axe because its handle was made of wood, they thought it was one of them.

Born, we were placed bareback under
the sun while crying, kicking
our feet as our cheeks
kissed the heat.

Melanin dripped all over us, forming
another skin. The torrid unsettling made us turn
over and crawl to their hushing.

We were cradled enough to find comfort
in their palms because their hands resembled ours.
We grew to fit into rumpled clothes
and tread around the dark chamber with locked bars.
We were happy to find shelter...

When it was time to eat, they shifted
their legs apart, but still, we crawled under
the table to nibble on fallen crumbs.
We stopped crying when our belly was half-full,
like sand grains in an hourglass turned over.

Our limbs became feeble from scrabbling
corners of the dusty walls with endless
hope for a key. They gave us walking
sticks to poke around and lessen the shaking.
We were happy about the support.

Our grave day was the noisiest.
Outside, barefooted on hard ground.
Kissed back at the sun, squinted eyes,
clanking of chains cuffed around our limbs.
We were happy...
Finally, we saw *them.*

Story for the Gods

I do not know a country
greater than my own...

It's a city of dry clay
guarded by silver and gold.
My town gate was forged from solid bronze.
House, cut from a century-old
Iroko tree, branches of the very first green.

Our mother is the goddess *Woyengi.*
She rode on thunderclaps, protected homes
with iron bars, sent serpents to fishermen's
streams, and maintained the ocean's blue sheen.

Our father is the red oil in our native soup.
He was painted on rocks that bedded
borderlines of our colourful tribes.

After our land was blessed with black oil,
we measured the miles of our day with clocks.
We no longer counted the setting suns
and chasing moons.
Because of this, our *Egbesu* faded,
weakening our defences.
Charcoal rained on crops and rivers,
covering the faces of welders as they fabricated
a third mainland bridge in a distant town.

***

Overlapping the lagoon and the island,
now our city is divided.
Elders sit on gold thrones
carried by gunmen on crooked roads.
They are chanting among themselves:
paper, paper, paper!

I do not know a country
greater than my own...

I Am Not My Brother's Keeper

My pockets are heavy from the stones they carry.
Coated with my brother's blood,
my conscience remains buried in mud.
Removed from his silent scream,
I do not flinch.

*

I was there when the doctor asked for a police report before
he could allow his stethoscope to test the pounding of your
chest—procedures that involve *not* saving lives.
He witnessed the shutting of your eyes,
the opening of your skull begging to be sewn shut.
The doctor was there! Just there, looking like *looku-looku*
with his hands folded and mouth covered by another man's hand.
He stared at you as you blipped like a sleeping
satellite wheeling away on this bloodbed.

*

I forgot my ears when the Pastor opened his house for you.
Dark clouds had overshadowed, and too many secrets became blind.
After the melody of clapping to the attention of his God,
you stayed behind.
Five men on your body, exchanging sweat in turns.
The Pastor removed his voice, but the rumours placed his body at the scene: They said he
plucked out his eyes to watch her legs quicken
and he removed his ears to hear her voice weaken,
with clothes ripped and palms pressing on white tears.
You did not understand the mystery of God's miracles.

*

I started sleeping on the edge of heated knives after an Officer's
machete tore open your back and exposed your spine to the desert.
Because you have never held a Quran, never kissed your head to the ground, or washed your
feet in a mosque, he slit your throat and cut off
your kneecaps, so you could not kneel and look up to the heavens
when you needed a god with a different name from Allah.
I wonder when your body was tossed away,
if the dusty winds carried your ghostly
whispers to merciful sands...

*

If the trumpet blows today,
I will say to God that there was nothing I could do except
record the last breath of another man;
give consent with my silence and gather more eyes,
because all my hands could carry was a video camera;
cut off my tongue to protect myself so I could not shout.
But I still pray that nobody shuts their mouth with sellotape
the day my voice is taken from me...

20 10 2020

#1

On the radio, they told us
to stay safe.
 *"There are no stray bullets
around Lekki toll-gate."*

The hairs at the nape of my neck stood up,
applauding to the trembles of a nation.
I had begun to realise people were dead,
with the national anthem bleeding
from their mouths.

They held on to the flag for dear life.
With legs and torso affixed and eyes
glued to my screen,

Looking at the boy who said:
        "Let them know how I died for my country."

Body riddled with bullets,
he shook like a leaf—
flighty like our constitutional rights.

I have learned that these rights exist only
when they are high up on cardboard
& broken banners,
wielded by broken hearts.

Nobody hears you until you cease to breathe.
& your father's cries echo around.
Your brother was stripped
naked and slapped for his right.

"We are the owners of the road,
and he is too young to drive on it."

I now finally understood what the dead
never said: patriotism here is
to die or to live.

#2

In today's political class, we were taught
ways to kill a mountain bird:
If it sings, plunge your fist through its throat
and pluck out its song.
Cut the wings;
never again will it flock and leave.
Or peck on words to assemble
a rabble or a desperate tweet.

Then, we were taught
to tame a snake:
Feed it with lots of paper.
Paper-cut from the national budget,
and pretend nobody saw it but you.
Explain there is no poison in money,
and those young tendrils can stop being so damn lazy.
Sell bleaching cream to Albinos and ice to the Inuit,
and leave daggers in the hands of pension-seekers.

The stress in governance is stressful,
and there is strength in breaking rocks from Aso-rock.
Make them chew down on stones
and pretend it's bread.

In today's class, we saw first-hand
that chess games
are for the brilliant
and politics are for those
who walk around with no hearts.

GHOST OF COVID

I wake,
acknowledging only my legs:
the rest of my body has abandoned me
& now on lockdown. My spirit has been ripped
out and raptured here to keep me company.
My brain sits on a table next to my computer
obsessed with creating lives outside
this encroaching box so I can exist.
Typing away, one hand attached to my keyboard,
the other grabbing a bottle of whiskey.
I crawl through, wording a fantasy of touch,
a meeting of snow and dust.
I play with them because my mind
    is free,

        roaming

                like this stupid virus

           eating up chunks of my lifespan

             & anatomy. I have transformed into
a vacuum, tethered to dusky legs & fidgeting fingers.

In this cocoon, there are no windows.
There is no difference between black to blue,
so I operate inside the dampness of dusk and dawn.
An eternal exchange of paper bags/ canned food/
dry mouth-liquor tongue /garbage room /& a screen
of numbers rising like the pile of dead bodies
spread across the news.
How do you kill a disease that teaches you
the politics of human proximity?

Days are compressed down to seconds &
I cannot understand the concept of clocks
anymore, but this tick is the only tok I talk to.
Suddenly I have become appreciative
of the stiffness of frowns & the consequence
of sleep—the softness of skin & the shinning of teeth.
Who knew that smiles could lift spirits so high,
like the smoke hovering around the ceiling
convincing you that there must be life in being a ghost?

When my brain fuel ruins out, I wander
back to bed, neck & torso resting. I wonder
where my head is at? I cannot remember
the feeling of being whole.

ACKNOWLEDGMENTS

The untitled piece on page 16 which opens this collection was shortlisted for the Bridport International Writing Prize (Poetry, 2022)